BOOKS I

RAINBOW

A STORY OF DAVID

by

NANCY LECOURT

Copyright © 1980 by
Southern Publishing Association

ISBN 0-8127-0290-5

This book was
Edited by Richard W. Coffen
Designed by Mark O'Connor
Illustrated by Betty Wind

Type set: 18/20 Century Schoolbook

Printed in U.S.A.

Southern Publishing Association, Nashville, Tennessee

Meet Rainbow.
Rainbow is a little lamb.
Rainbow is sweet and good, but not very smart.
Rainbow needs someone to take care of him.
Rainbow needs a shepherd.

Meet David.
David is a shepherd boy.
He takes care of Rainbow and Rainbow's family and all the other sheep.
He loves them all.

David is a good shepherd.
He leads his sheep to green grass.
He leads them to cool water.
He leads them to shady trees.
The sun can be hot on their wooly coats, so the sheep are glad to have a good shepherd like David, who finds them shade and water.

David also protects his sheep. He protects them from bears, and even lions!

And David sings to his sheep.

He plays a little harp and sings sweet songs.

He sings about the sun and the grass and the mountains.

And he sings about God.

David is so happy!

God gives him sun and grass and mountains—and a silly little lamb named Rainbow.

Every night David counts his sheep.
One, two, three, ...
David counts his sheep.

Tonight one is missing!
Who is missing?
It's Rainbow!
Where is Rainbow?
Where is that silly little lamb?

David must go back and look for Rainbow.
The wind is cold, the sky is dark, and David is hungry.
But he must find Rainbow!

David looks everywhere!
He looks by the river.
He looks by the tree.
He looks under a big rock.

"Rainbow! Where are you?"

"Dear God, please help me find Rainbow. He is so little, and the night is so big."

"Rainbow! There you are—you poor, silly little lamb! Caught in a bush!"

"I hope you've learned not to wander away from me any more. Stay with me, and you'll never get lost."

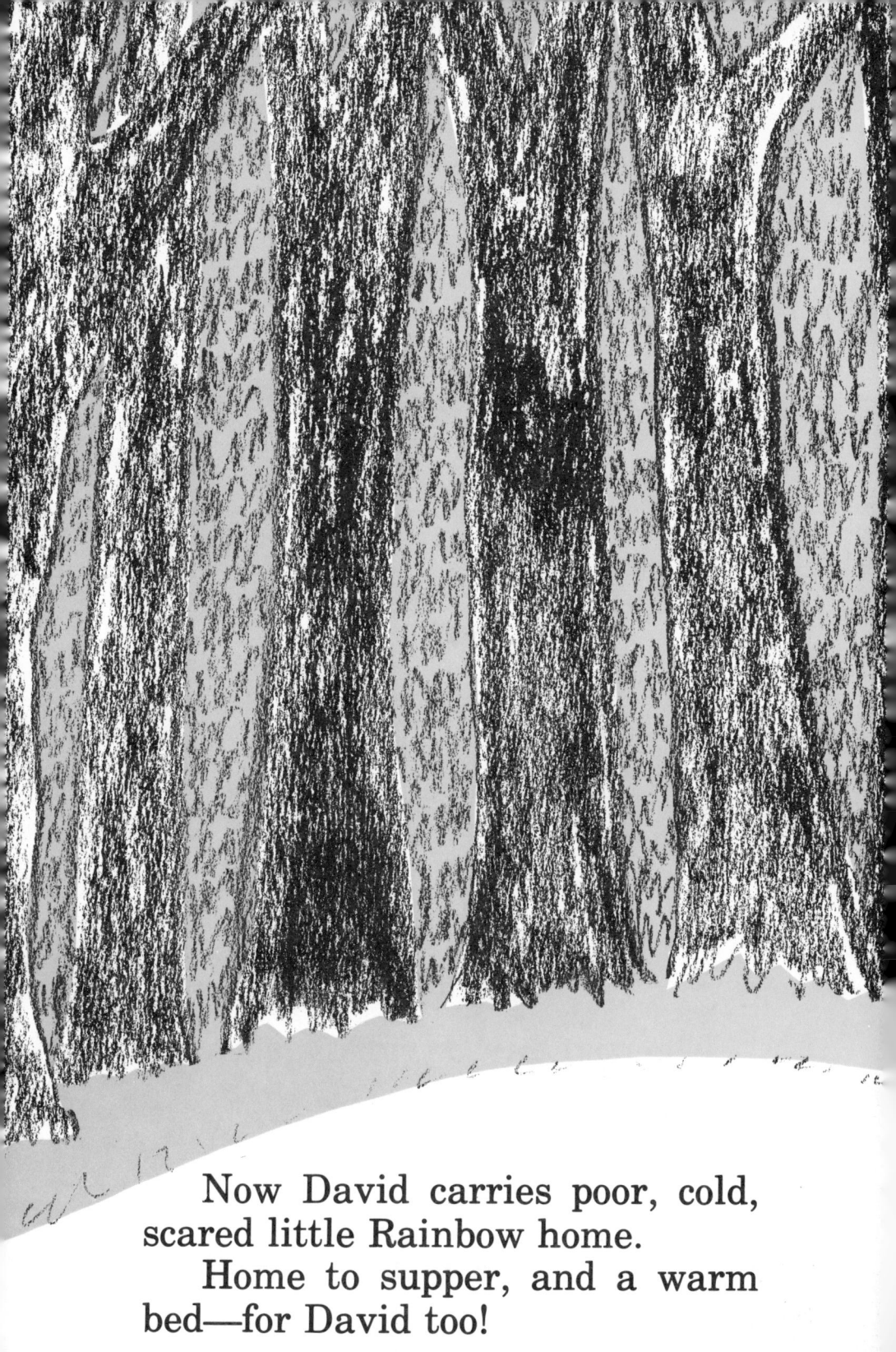

Now David carries poor, cold, scared little Rainbow home.

Home to supper, and a warm bed—for David too!

The next day David sings a new song.

"I am God's sheep,
And He gives me all I need.
He gives me good food.
And sweet water to drink.

"He gives me sleep at night. During the day He helps me do good."

"When I must walk in darkness
I am not afraid.
God is holding my hand!

"He is always there to protect me
and to guide me."

"Someday I will eat with God.
We will sit at a big table
And eat and drink and talk."

"I will live with God forever!"

Based on Psalm 23